Constitutional Authority
In a Postmodern Culture

Martin Murphy

Constitutional Authority in a Postmodern Culture

Published by:
Theocentric Publishing Group
1069A Main Street
Chipley, Florida 32428

www.theocentricpublishing.com

Library of Congress Control Number: 2015912965

ISBN 9780985618124

To my grandchildren living in this postmodern culture
Brad, Jon David, Savannah, Rebecca,
Mac, Carter, and Noah

Acknowledgments

Dr. Richard Pratt mentioned the word postmodern in a lecture in one of my seminary classes. The year was 1990 and I had never heard the word before. After the lecture I asked him to explain the term. He suggested I read *Postmodernist Culture*, by Steven Connor. I did and have read numerous other books on the subject since that time. Each one has helped me understand the concept and theories of postmodernism. I am especially thankful for Dr. Alasdair McIntyre, Dr. Gene Veith, Dr. Thomas Oden, Dr. J. P. Moreland, Dr. David Wells, and Dr. Richard Tarnas contributing to my understanding of postmodernism.

Table of Contents

1. Christian Living in a Civil Culture

The civil responsibility of the Christian is found in Paul's epistle to the Romans. It is there that the inspired apostle said of the Gentiles, "who show the work of the law written in their hearts, their conscience also bearing witness. . . . "(Romans 2:15). The *jus natura* (a system of natural law) calls every human being before the cosmic court to answer the charges of the Judge of the Universe. *The jus natura* is an allusion to the essential nature of man and explains why human beings have familial governments that collectively form governments in a larger society. This is nothing more than a Christian living in a civil culture.

The civil affairs of men are matters that concern the sphere of ethics and morality. Since the law is written on the heart, the law of God is binding on the civil magistrate (government) as well as the Christian. Obedience or disobedience to the law of God finally finds its end in justice. The basis of justice is authority. Moses declares to the people of Israel, "You shall appoint judges and officers in all your gates, which the Lord your God gives you, according to your tribes, and they shall judge the people with just judgment" (Deuteronomy 16:18). John Calvin said, "if it pleases God that judges should be appointed for ruling the people, it follows that their laws and edicts should be obeyed... ." Calvin goes on to say God, "Signifies that human society cannot hold together unless the lawful rulers have authority to execute justice. Whether, then, magistrates are appointed by the suffrages of the people, or imposed in any other way, let us learn that they are the necessary ministers of God, to confine all men under the yoke of the laws" (*Calvin Commentaries*, Vol. III, page 19).

The Bible does not explicitly mandate a form of government. However natural right theory so popular among the social contract advocates is anti-biblical. The political theory that gives the king divine right, although more sensible than the social contract theory is a weakened view of civil politics. The New Testament does not say obey the king, but it does say submit to the governing authorities. The question is whether or not obedience is absolute and final when the governing authority speaks. Dr. R. L. Dabney comments are apropos at this point.

> The government is for the governed, not for the especial benefit of the governors. The object of the institution, which God has in view, was the good of the community. The people are not for the rulers, but the rulers for the people. This is expressly stated by Paul, Rom. Xiii:3,4...The powers of the civil magistrate then, are limited by righteousness, (not always by facts) to these general functions, regulating and adjudicating all secular rights, and protecting all members of civil society in their enjoyment of their several proper shares thereof. This general function implies a number of others; prominently, these three: taxation, punishment, including capital punishment for

capital crimes, and defensive war. (*Systematic Theology*, by R. L. Dabney, page 865).

Peter and the other apostles were charged not to teach the doctrine of Christ, but Peter understood that there was a higher law to be obeyed. For that reason Scripture tells us "We ought to obey God rather than men" (Acts 5:29). When Christians were commanded by the governing authorities in Rome to worship idols, the Christians disobeyed. Christians are not bound in conscience to obey against the clear teaching of Scripture. The cultural shift that denies absolute truth as necessary for intelligent discourse will dismantle other aspects of a civil society. Postmodern theory treats truth much like the sophists: Truth is what they claim it is. Christians are commanded to render to Caesar the things that are Caesar's and to God the things that are God's. John T. McNeill wrote an essay on "Calvin and the Civil Government" in which he explained Calvin's view on this matter.

> Calvin realizes that government requires revenues and taxation. These funds are not the ruler's private incomes but belong to the people; they are in fact the very blood of the people and should be used in their behalf as a sacred trust, and not collected with rapacity or wasted in luxury. I conclude therefore that if the governing authority demands taxes for illegal purposes, the duty of obedience must be deferred to the Law of God. (Calvin and the Civil Government" by

John T. McNeill, *Journal of Presbyterian History*, Vol.42, p. 71)

Christians will always live in a civil society, but the culture will change. The beginning of the 21st century will experience a cultural change from modernity to postmodernity.

2. Constitutional Authority

I am not a civil jurist, but I have studied the Bible on the subject of authority and wrote a book titled, *Ultimate Authority for the Soul*. I believe the Bible provides principles relative to a constitution in relation to the governance of a state or nation. My only objective is to provoke some thought to the proposition of constitutional authority. The question that every citizen must answer: What is the authority for the establishment, maintenance, and enforcement of a constitution?

To make sense of this subject, we must agree to a common confession for the term "constitution." Every civil society must have a set of principles to govern the people. The word most commonly used to describe that set of principles is a constitution. The validity of a constitution may be argued based on a set of assumptions that range from social theories of government to philosophies of law. Any social theory of government must have a definitive plan to execute its agenda. Any philosophy of law must have a canon of ethics. The question is not which plan or canon is the right one, but what is the basis of the theory? To put it another way, what is the origin and basis for the mere existence of a constitution?

Sometimes there are movements that seek to change an existing constitution. The advantages and disadvantages of changing a constitution may become a major industry among the culture wars in that particular government. The immediate interest should not be who is right or who is wrong about the change. Changing a constitution often takes on the display of ignorance. It reminds me of Alice in Wonderland when the cat asked Alice where she was going? Alice answered and said, "I don't know." The cat responded, "then it doesn't much matter which way you go." If we don't know where we are going with the constitution, then it doesn't much matter which way we go? Rather than wrangling over the particulars of a constitutional change, the authority must lay a firm foundation upon which the constitution can rest. I want to examine several constitute parts of constitutional authority following what I believe is a logical order ascending from general principles.

The first general principle is human consciousness. The human conscience is the witness of an active force (Romans 2:15). Whether the conscience is conceptual or a component of the mind is a question for metaphysical inquiry. It is safe to say that most theologians and philosophers agree that the mind and the conscience are different entities. Jonathan Edwards' comment on the conscience is worth our attention.

> Conscience is a principle implanted in the heart of every man, and is as essential to his nature as the faculty of reason, for it is a natural and necessary attendant of that faculty. But the will of a wicked man is contrary to it, and inconsistent with it. They choose those things which they know to be evil, and ought not to be chosen; they choose that which their own reason

tells them is unreasonable and vile, and unbecoming men, and justly provoking to their Maker, and contrary to the end for which they are made. (*The Rational Biblical Theology of Jonathan Edwards*, by John Gerstner, Vol. 2, p. 245)

It goes without argument that the concept of self-awareness must be associated with the conscience. We cannot separate "self-awareness" from the mind or the will. The Bible teaches that the conscience indicates human responsibility associated with self-awareness. Therefore, the conscience must be the central self-awareness of the knowing mind and acting will communicated by human affections (emotions).

If what I've said is true, we cannot think of constitutional authority without considering the importance and the indubitable necessity of intelligent discourse. Again, I have to return to consciousness, which is foundational to the intelligent process.

Sometimes the human conscience convicts people by the reasoning they employ during the process of carrying on some kind of intelligent process. There are other times when the conscience excuses people even when they are guilty of violating God's law. There is either a little voice inside saying "what you're doing is bad" or it may say "what you're doing is good" even though in reality it is bad. If we understand as John Calvin did, "The law of God which we call the moral law is nothing else than a testimony of natural law and of that conscience which has been engraved upon the minds of men"

(*Institutes of the Christian Religion* 4.20.16), then natural law
and the moral law are the same. However the conscience is
part of the human nature which is a sinful nature therefore to
trust the conscience for infallible morality is indeed risky. If
we cannot trust our individual psychological self-awareness
and the authors of the constitution are conscious beings, then
what is the basis for constitutional authority? It must come
from principles derived from an infallible source.

The second general principle necessary to understand
constitutional authority is the concept of authority. *Black's
Law Dictionary* describes authority as that "power delegated
by a principal to his agent." Then there are several varieties of
authorities such as general authority, implied authority,
unlimited authority and so on. The question we have to ask is
this: Who is the "principal" and who is the "agent?" Let's put
the concept of authority in perspective using the example of
the president of the United States. He is said to have authority
to veto a bill passed by Congress. Who delegated the
authority to the president? The answer is simple; the
constitution gave him that authority. The answer is not
simple! Where did the constitution derive its authority? Is it
from the states or from the people? It does not matter, because
the concept of authority is lost in a whirlwind of legal jargon
among the cultural elites. With the demise of real, serious,
intellectual discourse by the infamous Immanuel Kant in the
18th century and subjectivized by Soren Kirkegard in the 19th
century, came also the demise of political, judicial, and
religious integrity. I am not prepared in this brief monograph

to give an explication of Immanuel Kant's theories on epistemology, but it is sufficient to quote the first sentence in the introduction of his *Critique of Pure Reason*: "That all our knowledge begins with experience there can be no doubt." Kant's individual psychological self-awareness was the final source of his authority. As I've already said self-awareness, consciousness if you will, is necessary, but the conscience is not the final authority since it is defective.

We are challenged by the work of Heinrich Rommen, a professor at Georgetown University from 1953-1967, when he said, "There is no soul, however corrupt it may be, in whom conscience God does not speak, if only it is still capable of rational thought. There are human actions, consequently, which are in themselves good or bad" (*The Natural Law*, Heinrich Rommen, p. 33). I mention Immanuel Kant briefly because of the tremendous widespread influence he has in the field of philosophy, religion, politics, and law. Kant's theory cuts out the concept of ultimate authority.

Let me call your attention back to *Black's Law Dictionary* where we find authority described as that "power delegated by a principal to his agent." The word "power" and the word "authority" are too often used interchangeably. For instance, in the Constitution of the United States immediately after the preamble we hear these words: "All legislative Powers herein granted shall be vested in a Congress of the United States..." Then throughout the constitution we find similar statements such as:

"The sole power of impeachment"
"The Senate shall have the sole power"
"The congress shall have power"
"The Executive Power shall be vested in a President"

By what authority does any entity have power? Authority does not depend on power, but to the contrary power depends on authority. I have often wondered why the drafters of the constitution did not begin with the recognition of some authority outside of itself. I expect it had to do with the abuse of rational philosophy and theology, an abuse that Immanuel Kant tried to correct.

It appears that many of the political leaders at the time of the drafting of the constitution were deists. Deism is the view that God created the world, especially the human rational faculties, but God is no longer personally involved in the governance of creation. The deist believes that God governs through unchangeable laws and that human reason is superior to supernatural revelation, particularly the miracles revealed in supernatural revelation.   Although there is some dispute among scholars, it has been said, and I agree that Thomas Jefferson, Thomas Paine, Ethan Allen, Benjamin Franklin and others were deists.   Is there any internal evidence in the Constitution itself to show the presence of Deism? I believe the answer is yes. Article Three, Section Two states, "The judicial Power shall extend to all Cases in Law and Equity, arising under this Constitution, the Laws of the United States, and Treaties made, or which shall be made, under their

Authority." The fallacy is that the power and the authority come from the same source. Like the Deists they violated the fundamental principle of causation. To put it another way proximate authority is an illusion without ultimate authority. We find ourselves going in circles trying to find out why authority is described as that "power delegated by a principal to his agent."

Maybe the confusion over power and authority is merely etymological. For instance in William Rawle's fine work on the constitution he refers to legislative power, executive power, and judicial power. Does he really mean authority or does he mean power? Under the heading of executive power he wisely observed that "In the formation of a republic there is perhaps no part more difficult than the right constitution of the executive authority." He rightly recognizes that authority is at the forefront of any constitution. I ask you to tolerate a brief excursus for the purpose of explaining the difference in the word power and the word authority.

The word "power" is derived from the Greek word *dunimis*. It originally referred to potential strength based on inherent physical, spiritual or natural powers. The English word dynamite is derived from the Greek word *dunimis*.When detonated dynamite will explode thus producing the action that is natural to the explosive.

The word "authority" is derived from the Greek word *exousia*. It literally means "out of being." The use of the word in both classical and *koine* Greek was in the areas of legal, political, social or moral affairs. For instance a king with authority may or may not have a powerful army. Therefore authority refers to a position, not an action. Unfortunately political philosophers, John Locke being one notable example, talk about authority in the hands of "the people at large," Another view contrary to Locke's view comes from Rev. Samuel Rutherford's work entitled "*The Law and the Prince*."

Rutherford posits "If all men be born equally free, as I hope to prove, there is no reason in nature why one man should be king and lord over another." He is not rejecting the concept of proximate authority as the Bible so clearly demands. Rutherford is talking about indiscriminate authority. In Paul's letter to the Romans he commands Christians, by inspiration from God to, "Be subject to the governing authorities. For there is no authority except from God and the authorities that exist are appointed by God."

For the sake of all those who are in the womb of their mothers and the young children who will have to live in a postmodern culture you should weigh carefully the concept of constitutional authority. There must be an objective standard, since human rulers are sinful and corrupt. The authority given human rulers is given by God, the Lord of all history and nations. The abuse of authority is tyranny. I'll let you decide if you feel tyrannized because of the abuse of authority from the hands of government leaders.

The effects of despotic power, guided and inflamed by the lust for power will oppress and finally imprison people like the nation Israel was oppressed and in bondage first to the Egyptians and then to the Babylonian government. Their suffering was the fruit of their ignorance of authority and submission to it. When King Nebuchadnezzar invaded the land of Judea, it was devastating for the people of God to be carried away in bondage. The Hebrew nation suffered the indignity because they rejected the ultimate authority of God.

The Hebrew nation was given a form of government over which God Himself was the Governor and King. It was a form of government with an objective standard that assured justice without oppression and tyranny. The people agreed with the law and freely adopted it. Then on occasions they would renew their covenant with God. The constitution they adopted, heavenly as it was, with all the promises of peace and prosperity, soon went by the wayside. They demanded a king, like the nations around them. They were not happy with their constitution, even though it came to them by ultimate authority. If we do not submit to the ultimate authority of heaven and earth, we will be like Alice in Wonderland. If we do not know which way we're going, it does not matter which way we go.

Now what should we do? The answer is simple. Adorn the civil constitution with moral truth from the ultimate authority. Wrap it with the kind of dignity you would expect from royal dignity. Appeal to the constitutional authority that will insure true liberty and real justice.

3. Metaphysical Neutrality in a Postmodern Culture

It was with purpose that our forefathers challenged the ignorance and incompetency of the ministry of King George III and later those same men would fight to the end for freedom from his tyranny. They decided the sacrifice was worth the result. Purpose is the motivating reason for every decision. Even co-belligerency has some purpose. I would not expect anyone reading this book to be opposed to the concept of God's sovereignty. If you had to choose freedom or tyranny, which would it be? If you had to choose between statism or a godly constitutional government, which would it be? Your choice follows your purpose. There is no in between; no adiaphorous. We are all slaves. We are slaves to our choices. You have a choice; you may be a slave to the state or you may be a slave to act responsibly toward a recovery of freedom and godly dignity. The wise man made it clear when he said, "He who is not with me is against me" (Matthew 12:30). Neutrality is not optional for those who pursue a godly purpose.

Neutrality is the phantom of egalitarianism. The word egalitarianism refers to the alleged equality of all rational beings. No society can be neutral and therefore egalitarianism is nothing more than the tyranny of a dysfunctional culture. The war zones in this country are proof that neutrality is impossible and egalitarianism is nothing but a front for those tyrants who want to micro-manage society. The wars I have in mind are not fought with guns. They are cultural wars fought on the battleground of the public arena. They are the battles fought over the family, art, education, law, politics, and interpretative theory. The clash began at the point when different people had different ideas about reality. The dispute is not over philosophical ideals. Quite to the contrary, the dispute is over who tells who what to do. For instance, the abortion issue is not a cultural war, per se. Neo-Christian ethicists, liberal politicians and judges are on one side of the abortion issue. Conservative Christians, the right to life movement, and orthodox ethicists are on the other side of the abortion issue. When the abortion pill, RU 486, was thrown into the arena for investigation the president of Planned Parenthood said, "If these drugs get to the market, the fight is finally over" (*Uncommon Sense*, by Cal Thomas). Although she made it sound like a battle, abortion is not a cultural war. Abortion is the catalyst that the cultural elites use to determine who controls the family, the court system, the political arena and the education of our children. These cultural wars are fought over authority and control. Where there is a question of authority, neutrality will never be found.

The attempt to define the American culture has not been an easy road to travel. The American way of life began with a clearly defined purpose. King George overlooked the determination of those men who were willing to sacrifice their fortunes and lives for a definitive cultural norm based on something greater than the incompetency and contumacy of a tyrant like King George. The fathers of the American culture fought and sacrificed for freedom from the tyranny of a dysfunctional monarch. Their purpose was to establish and pass on to the future generations a sense of dignity and a definition of their intentions, which they clearly stated in the Constitution. Unfortunately every generation tried to re-define those intentions with cultural modifications. It has been said that culture is relative to people and circumstances. Opening the doors to cultural relativity was the beginning of the cultural wars in this country. Although we speak of these cultural wars in terms of beginning around the mid-twentieth century, they have always visited us in one form or the other.

We never have been - nor will we ever be - nor should we be - free from debates in the public arena. The polarization of society demands intelligent discourse to resolve division when two parties maintain different sentiments. The process of this discovery is debate or disputation. It is never wise to concede to the old pseudo-peace slogan "Let's agree to disagree." However, the debates need a solid foundation, because real debates are concerned only about reality. The only solid foundation for reality must be metaphysical. We must look beyond this physical world if we expect to understand the world around us, the world we most commonly call our culture.

Metaphysics refers to questions of ultimate reality. However, postmodern theory rejects ultimate reality. Christian theology includes the study of the triune God and the soul of man, which are metaphysical. The soul is composed of, but not limited to, the intellectual, moral, and emotional aspect of our being. Metaphysical reality is the source of ultimate purpose. The proximate purposes such, as a bird having to have wings to fly is evidence for ultimate purpose.

If your cultural norms, your social standards, your economic objectives, and political proclivities are not grounded in a solid foundation, you will soon find yourself attempting to re-define your culture. In James Farmer's book titled *The Metaphysical Confederacy* he argues that "the concept of nationhood involves a zeitgeist around which a people can cohere" (p. 16). To put it another way, there must be some kind of agreement among the people in any given society. That does not mean that there is neutrality among the people. The agreement must have a substantial foundation so that, in the words of James Farmer, the "people can cohere." Farmer's thesis is that a metaphysical confederacy had to precede the physical confederacy. The metaphysical is reality and a confederacy coheres for a common purpose.

Most of us understand human suffering because we've experienced it, witnessed it, or read about it. People killing each other and destruction of property is as common as eating a meal. For those who miss the malicious suffering, there is hedonism, narcissism, and a whole host of other worldviews that travel the road of uncertainty. For many there is a sense of emptiness, because there is no understanding of ultimate purpose. I believe that the majority of theologians, philosophers, and political theorists of the antebellum era had a proximate purpose and that purpose was built upon the solid foundation of metaphysical purpose. The only foundation that will stand is the Christian Religion that our forefathers died to preserve. Although their progeny may be confused by the propaganda of the age, they still have the seed of perseverance planted in their hearts. There remains the hope to recover that metaphysical reality because there was and remains purpose behind the concept. I am convinced that without any metaphysical inquiry and without substantial agreement as a result of the inquiry, this nation will destroy itself. It is indisputably true that a house divided against itself will fall. Let me put your mind to rest that I am not insisting that a culture must perfect itself to stand against the tyranny of the elite. However, if a culture is not built on a sound foundation, it like any other edifice, the pilings will rot away.

A culture is simply a way of life. If we place the political and social aspects of a culture on a continuum, we might have two extremes: Cultural tyranny on one end or cultural anarchy on the other end. It is those two extremes that have given rise to the postmodern state. Modernity was very happy to fight over cultural issues such as education, politics or the family, so long as the gathered rational data or the scientific method could be used to measure the result of the battle. Fortunately for us the cultural anarchist could not agree with the cultural tyrant over the results of the test. For instance, one educator we will call the cultural tyrant may desire for you to turn your children completely over to the state educational system. Those educators, who are not educators at all, want to shape the children into social engineers, rather than educate them to be become productive thinking citizens. Another educator, we will call the cultural anarchist, has no interest in the education of the child. Those types of educators, who are not educators at all, have no agenda to produce intelligent productive citizens. One politician wants to shape society with his legislative applications while the other wants Washington to send his paycheck to his penthouse address in New York. Wherever the cultural battle is fought, we see the myth of neutrality and no solid foundation upon which to build cultural norms

Metaphysical neutrality has brought the American culture to a new crossroads. In the face of modernity's failure we find the emergence of postmodern theory. Alasdair McIntyre is a moral philosopher who brought the pendulum swing to our attention long before many others. In his book, *After Virtue* he said, "the enlightenment project failed." He is right in one sense of the word and wrong in the other. The failure of modern science and all its relatives has failed to give ultimate purpose to a secular world. However, I argue that modernity failed and another monster emerged. The failure of modernity has given rise to the postmodern. The modern man was driven to the edge of the precipice. However, instead of jumping off the cliff to find some relief, the postmodern simply emerged and refused to believe that there was a death trap at the bottom of the canyon. He wants to reshape all the ideas that drove him to the edge.

The postmodern culture will have nothing to do with the alleged absolutes of modernity. I suppose I have to say a few more words about modernity to bring my argument into focus. Modernity is more a concept than a period of time. The fourteenth century scholastics spoke of the *via moderna*, translated the modern way, long before the eighteenth century enlightenment. Yet there is a sense in which I agree with some scholars who believe that modernity raged from the storming of the Bastille to the fall of the Berlin wall. Modernity is the monster produced by the forces of its age such as hedonism, narcissism, pragmatism, and especially relativism. Now we hear philosophers talking about "the emptiness of the modern mind" because modernity failed to satisfy the soul of the culture. If urbanization, capitalism and technology, especially technology, failed to shape the culture then the postmodernist would say, "modernity failed." The blighted hope of the modern failure finds comfort, strange as that may seem, in postmodern theory.

Individual expressions of truth to the postmodern mind are simply nonsensical. I contend that the American culture drank deeply in the streams of postmodernity over the past 40 to 50 years. The evidence I present to defend my proposition is that postmodern theory rejects absolute truth. The result is we have a truthless culture. There is no metaphysic and neutrality has been crowned king.

"According to one poll 66 percent of Americans believe that there is no such thing as absolute truth" (*Postmodern Times*, Gene Edward Veith, Jr, p.16) in postmodern theory. To put it another way, the value of truth is personal relative.

When truth becomes personal relative then sophistry will
flourish in that culture.

> Sophistry is a subtle false argument. To sophisticate
> means to mislead by deception and false arguments.
> To be sophisticated is actually bad, although a revised
> contemporary meaning is that a sophisticated person is
> worldly wise, mature, classy, in the know, and on top
> of all situations. If the root word "sophism" is an
> enemy to truth, how can its derivative word
> "sophisticated" be good for truth? For instance,
> worldly wise does not necessarily express truth. (*The
> Dominant Culture: Living in the Promised Land*)

Human discourse will be meaningless. The postmodern
culture is not a demon to be tamed, but a cultural milieu that
must be replaced with a solid foundation that will grow a new
culture. There must be an objective standard for the new
culture, a standard that will survive cultural wars for the sake
of its progeny. Today your most formidable enemy is not
Washington D. C. as bad as they are. No, your most imposing
enemy is the postmodern culture that feeds Washington D. C.
If you don't remove the root that feeds the tree, you'll spend all
your time pruning the tree. Let me tell you from personal
experience, you will lose by attrition. If you do not understand
the postmodern concept I urge you to get Gene Veith's book
titled *Postmodern Times* or Thomas Oden's book *After
Modernity What?* If you really want to see how a liberal thinks

in terms of postmodern theory, I reluctantly recommend *Postmodernist Culture* by Steven Conner. The latter by Conner, who happens to be an English Professor, is a picture of the liberal agenda of the postmodernist. Would you like to know how the postmodernist thinks? Conner quotes Michael Ryan, another postmodern liberal from his work on postmodern politics.

> Rather than being expressive representations of a substance taken to be prior, cultural signs become instead active agents in themselves, creating new substances, new social forms, new ways of acting and thinking, new attitudes, reshuffling the cards of 'fate' and 'nature' and social 'reality'. It is on this margin that culture, seemingly entirely autonomous and detached, turns around and becomes a social and material force, a power of signification that discredits all claims to substantive grounds outside representation and this discrediting applies to political institutions, moral norms, social practices and economic structures" (*Postmodernist Culture*, p. 225).

Conner's "reshuffling" as he calls it, is the death of truth. The postmodern thinker posits, "there is no truth but my truth to my mind, and I'm sure that there is no truth but your truth to your mind." Therefore we must be multicultural expositors of the larger global community. The postmodernist would have you believe that truth is only meaningful to the author, speaker, or originator. We need to hear Mr. Liberal loud and clear. He said there is no solid foundation upon which we may build, "political institutions, moral norms, social practices and economic structures." Now I ask you, where will that lead your children and grandchildren? What will happen if there is no solid foundation for political institutions, moral norms, social practices and economic safeguards? I'll tell you what will happen. The culture will continue its endless drift through a maze of destructive ideas.

The postmodern theorist will redefine the author's words and terms. The postmodern interpretative twist has already poisoned the literary world, but can you imagine what will happen to historical interpretation in the generations to come? Historical revisionism will be normal. Postmodern theory will escort the American culture into a neo-dark age and its subjects will not realize what happened until it is too late.

I have not touched the aesthetic world in this discussion of postmodern theory. The disaffection of cultural norms has produced the uncontrollable meta-art in our day. The meta-art that comes out of Hollywood is more destructive than all the missiles China could produce. The entertainers are simply meeting the demands of the postmodern philosophers. Dr. Gene Veith has wisely said, "Postmodernist philosophers argue that all truth is a kind of fiction; postmodernist artists attempt to blur the distinction between art and reality" (*Postmodern Times*, by Gene Veith, p. 122). Myth and reality are easily distinguished if we have a solid metaphysical foundation. On the other hand metaphysical neutrality will easily accommodate postmodern conceptions.

If we understand the purpose of the liberal regime with its postmodern theory, we must turn our attention to the restoration and reformation of the church so it may affect the American culture. The foundation that I've referred to was once much stronger than it is now. The foundation will support the culture of dignity, respect, and moral accountability. The foundation laid by the founders of this nation was demonstrated by intelligence, dignity, and valor.

If you believe the once strong culture is worth recovering and preserving, it will require a passion for absolute truth. The popular has replaced the ideal. The postmodern concept has made its mark on everything from theology to quantum physics. It is my hope that we will all work hard to leave our progeny with the solid foundation necessary to build a lasting culture. Christianity alone is the way to defeat metaphysical neutrality in the postmodern world.

4. Celebrate Dependence Day

He who is the blessed and only sovereign, the King of kings and Lord of lords
-NASB

The blessed and only ruler, the King of kings and Lord of lords
-NIV

Only Almighty God, the King of kings and Lord of lords
-Living Bible
1 Timothy 6:15

King of kings and Lord of lords is a statement of God's sovereignty. Every king, president, governor, ruler and any other person in authority is subordinate to the great King and Lord of heaven and earth. They all depend on the sovereign King and Lord God Almighty. He has brought down rulers from their thrones" (Luke 1:52).

Just before the 4th of July each year television, radio, newspapers, internet and literally every form of communication writes or talks about celebrating Independence Day. It is my belief that Christians around the world ought to celebrate dependence day. These are a few thoughts to ponder relative to this important concept, commonly called independence.

As a national holiday, Independence Day, is the occasion to celebrate the absolved relationship between the thirteen confederated colonies and the throne of Great Britain. The despotic and tyrannical rule of King George III provoked the colonies to dissolve the relationship.

It is said that Thomas Jefferson was primarily responsible for drafting the declaration of independence. Thomas Jefferson's individualism is probably responsible for his use of the word independent.

You will not have to put forth much effort to discover the truth about Thomas Jefferson. He denied the authority of Scripture, the deity of Christ, and God's spiritual nature. In a letter to John Adams, Aug. 15, 1820 Jefferson said:

> To talk of immaterial existences is to talk of nothings. To say that the human soul, angels, god, are immaterial, is to say they are nothings, or that there is no god, no angels, no soul. I cannot reason otherwise: but I believe I am supported in my creed of materialism by Locke, Tracy, and Stewart. At what age of the Christian church this heresy of immaterialism, this masked atheism, crept in, I do not know. (http://www.let.rug.nl/usa/presidents/thomas-jefferson/letters-of-thomas-jefferson/jefl262.php)

For Jefferson, the existence of God equals nothing. Jefferson's religion was individualism. Jefferson's individualism emerged to become the most prominent religious view in western civilization. The formula for its success has an American and European contribution. From the American Revolution came "life, liberty, and the pursuit of happiness." From the French Revolution came "liberty, equality and fraternity."

Jefferson's declaration posits "We hold these truths to be self-evident that all men are created equal, that they are endowed by their creator with certain unalienable rights, that among these are: life, liberty, and the pursuit of happiness." An independent God gave the words life, liberty, happiness, equality and fraternity to dependent people. An individual or a nation will not acquire them without the generous hand of God.

Individualism is the predominant religion in the United States. This destructive religious view comes couched in terms like individual freedom and independence. It stresses the worth of self and individual ability to engage in political, social, and religious life. The individualistic independent worldview produces a democracy. Democracy literally means people rule. Democracy stands in opposition to theocracy. Democracy means "people rule" and theocracy means "God rules."

Is any person independent or any nation independent? The answer is no! God alone is independent. All existing matter depends on God's independency.

Am I advocating that the United States stop the great celebration every 4th of July? No! If I had been alive during the revolutionary war, I would have supported the separation from the tyranny of an ungodly ruler like King George. I would have called it separation from the British Throne day. I would also call for another celebration. "Dependence on God

Every day and Forever" which if put into practice would insure freedom from tyranny in the right sense. Paul told the philosophers at Athens what the people in the United States need to hear: "In Him we live and move and have our being" (Acts 17:28).

The Bible paints a vivid portrait of man's dependence on God. The spirit of individualism says, "I am," but God says, "I am!" Babylon, the great nation that ruled the world believed in the religion of individualism. A good example of the "I am" religion of this country in found in the book of Isaiah. The king of Babylon spoke arrogantly what most people keep to themselves; "I am and there is no one else besides me" (Isaiah 47:10).

How many times have I heard people, professing Christians, say, "pray that God will bless America." Why not pray, "God bless Iran, Afghanistan, and India? These countries need God to visit them with His grace and mercy just as He did the thirteen states that originally formed a confederation, but later changed it to a federation, commonly called the United States, however un-United they may be today.

The Bible is replete with words describing God as the only independent, necessary self-existent being. While King Nebuchadnezzar was flaunting his perception of independence, God reminded him of who really is independent.

King Nebuchadnezzar, to you it is declared: sovereignty has been removed from you, and you will be driven away from mankind, and your dwelling place will be with the beasts of the field. You will be given grass to eat like cattle, and the seven periods of time will pass over you, until you recognize that the Most High is ruler over the realm of mankind, and bestows it on whomever He wishes. (Daniel 4:31-32)

Every person will have to decide whether to celebrate the independence of God or the independence of self, or the independence of the United States. The only way to celebrate the independence of God requires an understanding of His nature and character. The concept known as "independence" belongs to God and to Him alone.

Another aspect of His being is simplicity and unity. God is not a compound being with various parts. Theological truth has practical applications.

There will be millions upon millions people who may otherwise believe in God, yet on the 4th of July they will try to steal a portion of God's unique character, his independence, and give it to the people who think they govern the United States.

Before I explain how that will happen, it will be necessary for us to affirm the independence of God. Then we affirm His unity. The Bible says, "God is spirit" therefore unlike humans He is not a composition of parts. God is one God. He is incapable of being divided into parts. Every nation is "divisible" but God's kingdom cannot be divided and God alone is "indivisible."

Now back to robbing God of His unique character. I am as guilty as anyone because I said it so many times when I would recite the pledge of allegiance: one nation indivisible.

Every nation on this planet is divisible. Every material substance is capable of division. Even the atom is divisible, even though it cannot be cut into pieces. God and God alone is indivisible. The independence and simplicity of God are not merely caricatures that misrepresent who He is. They are very real, but Christians often fail to recognize them.

Words have lost much ground in the wake of a culture that has crowned the queen of reality in terms of "image is everything." Words like independence, indivisibility, and united in a culture that is absolutely dependent and remarkably divided does not make sense. This country is divided by religious faith: Protestant, Roman Catholic, Baptist, Methodist, Presbyterian, et al. This country is divided politically: Republican and Democratic parties and many more. This country is divided over social issues that consist of a long list of cultural wars: Abortion, Law, and Education, to mention a few.

Many evangelicals believe Christianity has lost its influence in the western world. I interpret that to mean God's blessing has departed. It is not so much that God has departed. God has simply allowed individualism to rule in the land. It is as if God said, "You want to do it your way, have at it."

The doctrine is clear, the application is overwhelming, and so what shall we do? The answer is simple. Do what the Lord said to the nation of Israel many times over nearly 600 years of their history: return to the Lord! Returning to the Lord is something that happens every day. The first place to start is to know the Lord. He has revealed Himself in His Word. Rediscover His nature and character.

The first necessary step to overcome the Jeffersonian individualism and return to God is with the recognition that God actively provides for His creation. Eighteenth century Deism argued in favor of the generous providence of God. However, the deist said God is not active in the universe, especially among individual people. God created natural laws that give us life liberty and the pursuit of happiness. It is those laws that regulate life, not God's active hand.

The 309 million people in this country ought to celebrate God's generous providence. They ought to say this is the day that we depend on God for life and all the joy associated with God's blessing.

The doctrine of God's providence is the remedy for individualism.

Psalm 103:19 – The Lord has established His throne in heaven, and His kingdom rules over all.

Job 12:23 – He makes nations great and destroys them; He enlarges nations, and guides them.

The Bible explains God's providence in terms of His 1) sustenance 2) government 3) provision 4) concurrence.

Sustenance

What God creates he sustains. He holds all things together.
The universe and everything within it is dependent upon the
being and power of God for continuity of existence as well as
origin of existence. The Universe was not created and left like
a clock ticking away to point of expiration, as many deists
believe.

Government of God

God is the Supreme Governor who rules the world because of
his absolute authority and power to govern. When King
Nebuchadnezzar came to his senses he said that:

> God's dominion is an everlasting dominion
> His Kingdom endures from generation to generation
> His government is the directing and disposing of all
> things that come to pass.
> The adversarial disposition of man is to reject the
> government of God.
> Man rejects absolute authority.
> Man rejects the power of God.
> Common sense and the Bible tell us to respect the
> government of God because He provides.

Provision

God, whose foreseeing of all things is based on his foreordination of all things, is the provider who prepares a future for his people. Not only prepares a future, but meets all their needs. God provided the ultimate need of his people by sending his only Son to redeem his people. The ultimate provision was the substitutionary atonement to satisfy the wrath of God. The biblical pattern is that the Lord provides and His people are grateful.

Concurrence

God brings his plan to pass by His sovereignty through human means. For example, the sons of Israel sold Joseph into slavery. Later Joseph explained: And as for you, you meant evil against me, but God meant it for good in order to bring about this present result, to preserve many people alive" (Genesis 50:20).

Every aspect of God's providence are second causes, but God is the ultimate first cause. "And we know that God causes all things to work together for good to those who love God, to those who are called according to His purpose" (Romans 8:28).

Christians ought to take first things first. Do not undertake the study of any field of science until they understand the nature and character of God. Begin by studying these attributes of God.

His sovereignty

His independence
His simplicity and unity
His eternality
His perfections
His goodness
His truth
His holiness

Christians ought to thank God for His generous provision, His unwavering patience, and for giving us hope for the future. The hope for the future must be reformation, first in the church, and then take reformation into the culture.

5. Church Reforming the Culture

Reformation is derived from the word reform which is, "The improvement or amendment of what is wrong, corrupt, unsatisfactory, etc." (*Webster's Encyclopedic Abridged Dictionary of the English Language*). Christians may immediately think of the 16th century Reformation in Europe. However, reformation is an ongoing process practically used in every dimension of life. I want to apply the principle of reformation to the church and culture. For the Christian religion, reformation is always the church being reformed by the Word of God. Therefore, the source of reformation is infallible. However, the reformation will not be perfect because of the sinful nature of the people involved in the reformation. The source for cultural reformation is fallible, unless the Bible is the source for the standards for reformation. Jonah 3:1-10 describes a cultural reformation.

Cultural derives from the word "culture" which refers to a particular way of life for a designated group of people. For instance the southern culture in the United States is a way of life distinct from the northern culture. The word reformation denotes a change from one way of life to another way of life. The book of Jonah depicts the true nature of reformation in the most universal sense. There may be a few preachers who actually talk about reformation, but they do not appear to take reformation very seriously. When they do talk about reformation they are more often concerned with constraint and circumscription's that limit reformation. Biblical reformation is the discovery or either the recovery of biblical truth. Since reformation is the recovery of biblical truth, Christians should hasten to bring it about. Recovering the truth of the law and gospel is ultimately important for the survival of any culture, because such recovery integrates dignity and moral standards.

Some people are getting ready to die because of age and corruption. The babies coming in this world are getting ready to live. What will we devolve on the shoulders of our children and each succeeding generation, if we do not seriously and sincerely seek reformation in the church and culture, thus affecting every area of life including our religious, familial, social, economic, and political lives? An insincere reformation is no reformation at all.

Jonah reflects the principles necessary for reformation in church and culture. Being reformed by the Word of God is necessary to grasp the substance and essence of life. To ignore reformation is dangerous indeed, because without reformation God's wrath will be provoked.

You might say to yourself, "I don't want to provoke God" at least I hope you would entertain that thought. You don't want to provoke God and yet evil is provocative. There is such a thing as a provocative prophecy.

> When you begat children and grandchildren and have grown old in the land, and act corruptly and make a carved image in the form of anything, and do evil in the sight of the Lord your God *to provoke Him to*

anger, I call heaven and earth to witness against you this day. (Deuteronomy 4:25)

Doing evil provokes God to anger. Let me give you a couple of examples from the Word of God.

(After the death of Joshua) Then the children of Israel did evil in the sight of the Lord, and served the Baals; and they forsook the Lord God of their fathers, who had brought them out of the land of Egypt; and they followed other gods from among the gods of the people who were all around them, and they bowed down to them and they **provoked the Lord to anger.** (Judges 2:21)

Do you see this, son of man? Is it too light a thing for the house of Judah to commit the abominations which they have committed here, that they have filled the land with violence and **provoked me repeatedly.** (Ezekiel 8:17)

From 1450 B.C. to 600 B.C. the people of God provoked God to the point that His glory departed from the temple in Jerusalem. It was symbolic of God's favorable presence leaving the people who professed to believe Him.

The people in Sodom tried neutrality. It didn't work. When the wicked men of Sodom were told of the eminent destruction they just couldn't believe it was true. The nearness, the uncertainty, greatness and eternity of God's punishment and wrath doesn't seem dreadful or miserable for the unreformed man. Natural man *cannot* be reformed and wicked men *will not* be reformed, but those whom God has called to Himself can and must seek reformation. The choice is simple: reformation or judgment.

In a brief but compelling prophecy, Jonah and the object of his prophecy exemplifies the simple choice I just mentioned: reformation or judgment. In chapters one and two Jonah was reformed by the mighty hand of God. Jonah's personal reformation required a little encouragement, but he finally got the message and found that reformation was better than judgment. In chapter 3 the principles of reformation were on the thoughts, tongues, and lives of the Ninevites.

I grant that the reformation in Ninevah was not permanent. Every generation must seek reformation according to the Word of God. It was for that reason that the 16th century Reformation reformers used the Latin phrase:

"ecclesia reformata semper est reformanda"
"The church reformed is always being reformed"

In the context of the 16th century Reformation, it was understood that every generation was being reformed by the Word of God. Every Christian and every generation must rediscovery the truth of the Word of God, so the beauty, majesty, and dignity of God will be the basis for culture.

After Jonah's personal reformation he went to preach reformation to the whole city of Nineveh or to put it in other terms Jonah preached to a culture unfamiliar with the true and living God.   Jonah went through the streets of Nineveh preaching a very simple, but very persuasive sermon. "Yet forty days, and Nineveh shall be overthrown" (Jonah 3:4). John the Baptist preached much like Jonah.   They both preached repentance. Apparently Jonah's preaching was very powerful and very convincing, because the whole city repented in sackcloth and ashes. It was an act of humility and indicated a change of heart. The church (represented by Jonah) had a good effect on the culture (represented by Nineveh).

The repentance at Nineveh was universal and was occasioned by their faith in God. The unexpected, but sudden reformation at Nineveh began with the people and very quickly reached the heads of state. The undeniable truth from the book of Jonah is that the reformation at Nineveh saved that city from God's impending judgment. "Then God saw their works, that they turned from their evil way; and God relented from the disaster that He had said He would bring upon them and He did not do it (Jonah 3:10)."   The sinful people at Nineveh were about to have the wrath of God poured out upon them.   But God showed mercy after the people of Nineveh were reformed.

God will often show mercy to sinful people by warning them of His approaching judgment. God warns people of His coming judgment by means of sending a natural catastrophe, sickness, or other providential intervention that should get their attention. It seems to me that God's warning comes in an ascending order. When we think of the final destruction of Jerusalem in 586 B. C., we have little regard for the numerous lesser warning that the Israelites received beginning nearly 400 years before God's fury fell mightily on Mt. Zion. Sometimes God warns His covenant people by warning other people around them with more severe judgments. The captivity of the northern kingdom of Israel was sufficient to awaken the sinful ungodly southern kingdom to repentance. But Judah would not reform and so God's judgment fell upon Judah.

Another way God warns people of His impending judgment is to send a messenger. God has sent many a messenger to warn his people. Just as God sent Noah, Moses, Samuel, Elijah, and whole host of other prophets, God has called and sent his ministers to warn first the church and then the whole world. I am not able to prophesy the particular time or the particular manner of God's coming judgment, but I may apply God's warnings according to God's Word and His providence. When we hear of a great natural catastrophe, we should think of God's judgment. You might be inclined to believe that a hurricane destroys life and property because of the atmospheric conditions that occur naturally. That is bad thinking. A hurricane exists because of sin. Before sin entered into the world there could not have been destruction, death, and disorder. In a perfect world there is harmony and peace. A hurricane is God's judgment, just like sickness is God's judgment, just like death is God's judgment. Christians must not be ashamed of the same kind of preaching that accompanied reformation at Nineveh. "Yet 40 days and Nineveh will be overthrown." To try to hide the threats of God is like trying to hide from reality.

The lesson from Jonah and Nineveh is reformation and people turning from their evil ways will avert God's threatened judgment. Not only from Jonah, God spoke through the prophet Jeremiah and said, "The instant I speak concerning a nation and concerning a kingdom, to pluck up, to pull down, and to destroy it, if that nation against whom I have spoken turns from its evil, I will relent of the disaster that I thought to bring upon it" (Jeremiah 18:7).

God not only calls the church to reformation, but God calls nations to reform. Once the church has recovered the truth of God's grace, the church must then take that truth to the culture. Our present national sins should be of great concern to the church. Today God's people feel the threats of every international, national, and local crisis that erupts. We sense the coming economic calamity. We see the moral catastrophe that accompanies a form of godliness among many professing Christians.

Since reformation is absolutely necessary for the church and culture what must God's people do? Let's get together and pray. I tell you that will not bring reformation. Let's have a day of fasting. Again fasting will not bring reformation. Let's have a revival service. No. No. No. Prayer and fasting is good and necessary, but they are not the instruments of reformation. A revival service without reformation is useless.

The people of Nineveh believed the Word of God. This is the central principle of reformation: "they believed the Word of God." Then they fasted. Like Jonah, you'll have to experience personal reformation first. Rediscover God's truth. The light of God's truth will light up a passion for reformation that will work itself out as a revival.

The well intentioned Christian may say, "We know of God's impending judgment, but preaching God's judgment will chase people away and we'll never get to save them." It is correct no one can save anyone, but God does save people and He uses His Word to convict them of their sins. When the "Lord opened her [Lydia's] heart to heed the things spoken" she was able to believe and seek reformation from the written Word.

The majority of the church and most of our nation has not given attention to the terrible threats of God. Multitudes of sermons have been preached about reformation and the imminent dangers if people continue unreformed. Those sermons have largely been ignored. God is angry with the gross hypocrisy and the great heresies that plague the professing evangelical church. The church will do well to listen to God's threat of judgment. The church will do well to cut out all the talk about reformation, and stop amusing themselves with egocentric worship. Talk and self-worship will find its end in God's judgment.

The present condition of Christianity is that it suffers from a lack of understanding God's nature and character. The result is that the doctrine of salvation tends toward a form of man-centered universalism. The present unreformed church simply refuses to preach the simplicity of God's grace, man's sinful condition and in particular the doctrine of God's salvation.

It seems the fundamental doctrines such as God's justice and love have been distorted. With so much backwards theology, Christians must recover the full counsel of God, if we expect reformation in the church extending to our culture. Reformation will come when Christians:

1. Seek God's counsel from His Word.
2. Hide God's Word in the heart's mind.
3. Declare God's Word without shame.
4. Delight in the Word of God and never forget it.

Reformation for the church is the recovery of biblical truth. Natural man cannot recover biblical truth. Wicked men will not recover biblical truth. Since God's covenant people are the instruments of reformation, they must take the reformation into the culture.

"We are accused of rash and impious innovation, for having ventured to propose any change at all on the former state of the Church" (*The Necessity of Reforming the Church*, by John Calvin, Works, vol. 1, p.125). Calvin used two interesting words that aptly describe reformation. The word innovation from the Latin *innovare*, "to renew" was needed in the day of Calvin and it is needed today. The church does not need a new gospel or a new way to worship, but it does need to restore the gospel and the orthodox way to worship which has been trampled upon over the past couple of centuries. Innovation describes the work of reformation and change describes the result of reformation.

Michael Horton argues that "theology, not morality, is the first business on the church's agenda of reform, and the church, not society, is the first target of divine criticism" (*Beyond Culture Wars*). Innovation begins with theology and ends with theology. Paul the apostle said, "I press on to take hold of that for which Christ Jesus took hold of me" (Philippians 3:12). Paul strived for an understanding of righteousness, peace and the knowledge of Jesus Christ, which is essentially and practically theological. Paul's innovation rested squarely on a theological framework. A reformer is innovative only when he or she has a passion for believing and living according to God's standard as he or she is enabled to believe and live by the power of the Holy Spirit.

The meaning of reformation and thus what it means to be a reforming Christian has been forgotten, because the evangelical church has turned her back on the foundational doctrines of the Christian faith. The evangelical church has replaced the law and the gospel with human-centered structures that meet "felt needs" those that are "user-friendly" and are "seeker sensitive."

At the beginning of the 16th century Reformation Martin of Basle came to understand the truth of the gospel, but he was afraid to make a public confession. He wrote these words on a leaf of parchment: "O most merciful Christ, I know that I can be saved only by the merit of thy blood. Holy Jesus, I acknowledge thy sufferings for me. I love thee! I love thee!" He removed a stone from the wall of his chamber and hid it. It was not discovered until a hundred years later.

About the same time Martin Luther discovered the truth and he openly confessed: "My Lord has confessed me before men; I will not shrink from confessing Him before kings." The Reformation continued and we remember Martin Luther for his devotion to innovation and change, but what about Martin of Basle? Who was the reformer?

Innovation is that aspect of reformation that seeks to recover the integrity and dignity of the Christian religion. Our forefathers suffered and died for the integrity of the gospel and with dignity they have passed on to us the torch of reformation.

Calvin left us with these words and I leave them with you: "But be the issue what it may, we will never repent of having begun and of having proceeded thus far. . . . We will die, but in death even be conquerors. . .because we know that our blood will be as seed to propagate the Divine truth which men now despise" (*The Necessity of Reforming the Church*, by John Calvin, Vol. 1, p. 234.).

About the Author

Martin Murphy has a B.A. in Bible from Columbia International University and Master of Divinity from Reformed Theological Seminary. Martin spent nearly thirty years in the class room, the pulpit, the lectern, the study, and the library. He now devotes most of his time consolidating academic and practical gains by writing books. He and his wife Mary live in Dothan, Alabama. He is the author of twelve Christian books.

The Church: First Thirty Years, 344 pages, ISBN 9780985618179, $15.95. This book is an exposition of the Book of Acts. It will help Christians understand the purpose, mission, and ministry of the church.

The Dominant Culture: Living in the Promised Land, 172 pages, ISBN 970991481118, $11.95. This book examines the culture of Israel during the period of the Judges. It explains how worldviews influence the church and it reveals biblical principles to help Christians learn how to live in the culture.

My Christian Apology, 98 pages, ISBN 9780984570874, $7.95. This book investigates the doctrine of Christian apologetics. It explains rational Christian apologetics.

The Essence of Christian Doctrine, 200 pages, ISBN 9780984570812, $12.95. This book was written so that pastors and laymen would have a quick reference to major biblical doctrines. Dr. Steve Brown says it was written, "with clarity and power about the verities of the Christian faith and in a way that makes a difference in how we live."

Return to the Lord, 130 pages, ISBN 9780984570805, $8.95. This book is an exposition of Hosea. The prophet speaks a message of repentance and hope. Hosea's prophetic message to Old Testament and New Testament congregations is, "you have broken God's covenant; return to the Lord." Dr. Richard Pratt said, "We need more correct and practical instruction in the prophetic books, and you have given us just that."

Theological Terms in Layman Language, 130 pages, ISBN 9780985618155, $8.95. This book was written so that simple words like faith or not so simple words like aseity are explained in plain language. Theological Terms in Layman Language is easy to read and designed for people who want a brief definition for theological terms. The terms are in layman friendly language.

Brief Study of the Ten Commandments, 164 pages, 9780991481163, $10.95. This book will help Christians discover or re-discover the meaning of the Ten Commandments.

The Present Truth, 164 pages, ISBN 9780983244172, $8.95. Each chapter examines a topic relative to the Christian life. Topics such as church, sin, anger, marriage, education and more.

Doctrine of Sound Words: Summary of Christian Theology, 423 pages, ISBN 9780991481125, $16.95. This is a book of Christian doctrine in topical format. It covers a wide range of theological topics such as, the triune God, creation, providence, sin, justification, repentance, Christian liberty, free will, marriage and divorce, Christian fellowship, et al). There are thirty three topics beginning with "Holy Scriptures" and ending with "The Last Judgment." It is a systematic theology for laymen based on the full counsel of God.

Friendship: The Joy of Relationships, ISBN 9780986405518, 48 pages, $6.49. This is the kind of book that friends give each other and share the principles with each other. If friends do not feel comfortable sharing these relationship principles with each other, the friendship may not really exist. Friendship involves a relationship of distinction. It is a relationship that respects the dignity of another person. The Bible teaches a different version of what it means to be a friend than the popular culture teaches. There are many occasions when friends say they are friends, but they are not friends. "Even my own familiar friend in whom I trusted, who ate my bread, has lifted up his heel against me" (Psalm 41:9). A true friend will endure and sacrifice for a friend. "A friend loves at all times" (Proverbs 17:7) and "there is a friend who sticks closer than a brother" (Proverbs 18:24).

Ultimate Authority for the Soul, ISBN 9780986405501, 151 pages, $9.99. What is the ultimate authority for human beings? This book examines that question and concludes that every rational being has some recognition of God as the ultimate authority. Although God is the ultimate authority, He confers His authority by means of the Word of God. The author examines Psalm 119 to build a defense for the ultimate authority for the soul. Although this book was written for Christians, the author builds the case that authority is a principle necessary to maintain sanity and order in the family, the church and civil society. The Word of God connects the soul with reality.

www.ingramcontent.com/pod-product-compliance
Lightning Source LLC
Chambersburg PA
CBHW060724030426
42337CB00017B/2994